Ram Hands

Ellen Welcker

Published by Scablands Books
scablandsbooks.org

ISBN-13: 978-0-9907525-4-7
ISBN-10: 0-9907525-4-2

Managing Editor: Sharma Shields
Editor: Maya Jewell Zeller
Cover art and book design: Keely Honeywell

Printed in Spokane, WA by Gray Dog Press

eider ducks, spiders, and vinegar
exist, and the future, the future

—Inger Christensen, from *Alphabet*

Contents

I. My Ram Hands

II. Mouth That Tastes of Gasoline

I. My Ram Hands

This Day in History

Step one was chop onions.

Step two was make a bed so cauliflower can nap; this was before I knew that one lady was a fraud. My feeling was, then and now, real.

I'd been conducting a seminar on the female experience. We began with a boiled egg—attendance was spotty—followed by a round of self-flagellation with a variety of kelp.

Ground rules included prohibition of circulation because no pain no. This was, after all, a female experience. Very. Gainsayers were everywhere. When numbness set in, the rush of blood like a flood forced new chutes through everyone's topographies.

These channeled scablands were deemed Zoticist Channels™, "life-giving," from the medieval Latin *zoticus*, a root word which, unuttered all this time, had shrunk from its nutrient-seeking finger, leaving, of course, a Hole. The people cooed and cried; though hardly in the past, experientially, it was already lore on their tongues. The Hole was an expert in her field, had been burrowing for centuries, had calcified, bled, leaked, cracked, grown sour, and soft as compost again.

The Hole flicked open a compact, held the mirror to her open mouth, motioned for us to gather round. We peered for hours, alternating between the darkness of her interiority and the relief of the steaming glass. Slowly we saw she was a wormhole, a channel to the future, tunnel that hadn't happened yet, inverse of a black hole. So dense with matter.

I said to it, for "it" was genderless, a-gendered, a genderhole: *I'm with you, I'm right here.* It said, *No. Come in.* Inside that vowel, that "I," was a pink tunnel. It had a beginning (false), and an end (made-up). It was narrative.

"Lair," the tunnel preferred to be called, "Den." "Hole," people called it anyway, "Hole." The tunnel that was a poem, a country, a lie, or rather— a shaft of stolen thoughts. Some of them still glittering, like ore.

Finally, we arrived at a small appendix, flaccid, pure cliché—but once it had been taken at its word. Once, it had held breaths in its belly, kept them, and grew, 'til it was no longer a button but a globe: huge, resplendent with air, deer, splinters, carpets, blooming tick populations, celebrity endorsements, humidity, toxic shock syndrome, unidentified pestilences, clouds of spores.

Things were about to get real, my friends. I blew my nose. My hair product was sheer intensity. The cauliflower was just getting woke.

Rhetorical Analysis

Of sea-wolves
and people swapping bodies for cosmetic reasons
which is the more feral?
Even a baby could answer that, so try
to be more feral, feral as rain
which is what I picture
when people talk about micro-aggressions:
a pelting, unceasing rain
and a coat that appears to be made of white feathers
but is obviously toilet paper.
You are soaked and this disintegrating coat
will dry and suck
all the moisture from your skin, which is aging
more rapidly than you could have imagined.
"Everything officially human lies above the cerebral cortex."
Do we think this means our humanness
is situated in our minds
or do we think this means everything
human is deceitful? If the latter,
we must toss the phrase, "in my heart of hearts."
We must remember that feeling is animal.
When you're being hunted, you might watch
your stalker; stillness is your weapon.
Here's another tip: don't toss your keys
in the ditch and then run for your car.
Is it or is it not interesting
how poison is so close to *poisson*
how "management" is a euphemism
how "wildlife" is a funny word
ripe for punning, a tossup
for bosses, "Spawn
or Die," over beers—
a slogan so already better
than this muddy water
in the mouth of the utterer.

ellenwelcker, you have no events scheduled today

ellenwelcker, you have no events scheduled today.

ellenwelcker, you have plenty of time
to have neoplastic dreams, ellenwelcker.

click on five signs
you will get cancer

think slick thoughts
about confession, ellen

like, if you can give me
like me, if you can

mammalian heat & a slick thought
a blind hopping or slipping

like can you give an evasive one
this might be the ticket, & tenderer

ellenwelcker, possibly
you are some percentage red #5

possibly you strain to separate your you
from the super, mega, googly-store

brim to brim with the bad-bad, & sad sad-
ness is a radial emotion echolocating

big ass pile of laundry blocking my sun
can you give an evasive one

can you closetalk in small spaces,
intimate, soft spaces

palpate palpate your tumors
& yous

a poet is like a bat
intertextual & cavey

& nothing, I mean no percentage
learning to "cope"

Nature Poem

Let's say you're a female animal
and a parasite has infected your brain,
made you do crazy things. Let's say
it's not living inside you, exactly,
but near you, near enough to come
inside you, dripping poison,
though let's say it's not poison,
but a magic elixir that mixes
with yours, begins to grow. See
how out of control things
can be? Let's say you're not
a woman, exactly, but female,
a female animal, and someone,
another animal, wants to nest
inside you. She looks around
for someplace to get in and
when she does, she leaves her body
behind: now she has yours.
Her nest might look like a tumor
hip-checking for wiggle room, hungry
for your food. The animal renders
your sex organs useless and you care
for the children of this shadow-you. Now
she bores a hole in you: makes a new
cunt, where they can come
to mate with her through you,
an animal, too.

A Book About Georgia

her mountain—where her ashes are—*being burned!* the big one
      bellows
that's what she calls it and that's what it is

I am like a black match, or a piece of old wood, cold in the stove—
      you can't
feel it you can't feel it you're already dead I say

I thought dying was only being buried, she bellows and I don't know
why that's better—are you enjoying this conversation

I ask a concentrated beam of matter, they
grip at my skin and hair—*if I die will you come with me*

bellows the big one and for the very first time the little one cries
I don't want to! I will put this in his baby book

I think, next to the envelope of blond wisp—the beam of matter
      says it's a wonder
we do anything but cry about death

while we're alive *hush* I say *hush* you are eating all your snap peas
and that's the very best that you can do

A white cry brought the morning to its feet

I believe there are vultures circling me

their shadows criss-cross my body

sweat drips from my body   onto my body

last year I wore a down vest

this year it just looks at me

        maybe

you've seen me   *tell the roots*

I want to go deep into something deep

not this deprivation   not this debt

maybe we're not allowed to write about anything else

not while we're still frothed   at the gap

      not while everything is

a weapon   I walk with

my weapon   a tool makes me

one

      to put a girl   in various quotes

to melt her   'til she is nothing

but her liquid   or worse

the feeling of falling   is like nothing

it is nothing   *the medulla of air*

these various airs

their thumblike thickness or   wilder

ness   feeling of falling

is nothing   I am smiling

at nothing   really smiling   at nothing

I was speaking that way   but wishing

I could speak another

when I fall   let me suck the sky

not for fear or anticipation   or to buoy

or to protect   but to take blue in my body

as I've done so often & thought

     lessly   it is the way of us

anyway, I know   and anyway

I know nothing

     I was speaking that way   and I wanted

to speak another way   maybe

we're not allowed to write about anything

else   not while we are still   writhing

racists   in a new way

a slightly different way   this is no way

                  at all   It's a shame

I know intimately

that everything wants to become something else

so many lamenting cows   so many

lamenting cows   sick and dying cows

and bellowing   and wrung dry

like the wallpaper I eyed   leaned closer   blinked

yellowed   *the cow of ash*

                        molded from ground

beef   and photographed

for the cover of a magazine

tell the roots

now   they can eat the cow   now

that my skin strives   for dust

that my tears and sweat find the sea

eventually   that my scratches long to be claws

and my glistening organs   pearls

nestled in the thick muscle of a saltwater

clam   surrounded

Tools

I took my scythe to the bathroom. The vibration was scary, almost. I couldn't wait to get out of there. Some of us were standing around with our tools; others of us immediately took to hacking and battering the ground and nearby bushes.

After a time of holding it awkwardly, I hinged at the elbow to rest the backside of the blade on my shoulder. I had a conversation and my scythe became a credential, an integral part of an unspoken power dynamic. The slightest stem of grass leapt from my blade.

After a while I traded it for what I thought was some sort of air gun, but was actually a blowtorch. It had a long hose that I looped confidently over my shoulder. The urge to faux-lasso was strong. The urge to become a joke, human + tool, or was it woman + power tool? The joke. I swung it around, became embarrassed, lurched aimlessly on my feet. My feet like two clubs: dumb weapons. I didn't have a flame canister. I felt like a child.

My pickaxe was in someone else's hands. They drove it again and again into the gravel road. My breath coming short, wet, hot.

I tried to think of something to say. In my mind I scrolled through celebrity tools, tools of the founding fathers, tools of religion and self-defense, ordinary tools. I did a small eccentric dance with my handsaw.

It came to me, suddenly, then, like a shot, like a person who wears a lover with no one inside.

I held my sling at the crux of the Y. I aimed at the sky. The sound was appealing when I hit the overturned trough, but I preferred the lob of earth arcing through blue.

Back in the bathroom, I'd seen a sign, impossible to read, wasn't it? When I came out—the looks of shock on our faces—the tools with their brains, still throbbing in our white-knuckled hands.

poem that wonders if it feels safer with a blanket over its head

eating is bloody
living is expensive

in which a woman in which
a rage in which a sex joke

in which satiation isn't
in which to kill is

a furry burr in brains
a chunk of nickeled days

a shuffle in which relations
a moral in which the milk

being children won't do
the nameless runts

the howl
the cunts

to be digested
rather than shot

to be disappeared or left
in the street

to be the butter "all gone" or
not to be butter at all—

there is a beast
who wants to learn you

it wants more suckage
it wants more froth

you wash
you wash your hands

they still smell
still smell they still smell

My Brand

I'm sorry, Darigold. Your cow is no good here.
Look at that cute famine on the horizon
fluffily disguised as homage
to a motherland not our own, &
weirdly appropriated in the synapses
of our affection. Unmanaged, mommily,
& valved as the veins of bovines;
ore-ish as their petty liquid spilt.
I'm yodeling when I think about my brand—
I'm like, WINTER IS COMING, but then, I'm
a forgettable mammal, uddered
& tailless, fucked & machinated & sold.

Still Life with Viewer as Object

The tonight is fact.
Under the blanket of which
I did not go. With the performance artist.
Woman accused of sleeping with the entire boy band.
Woman pretending to be furniture.
I can see you are not damning.
As soon as possible
will you give one, and hon—
be a lot more fun and addicting.
Bring home a nickname tonight
like, One Who Tenderly Runs One's Fingers Through Hair,
Cootie-Free.
My bone screws are hurting. It's sockeye
to suckerpunch up in here and I don't think
you think I think this isn't true.
Woman on the cover of *Vogue* wearing nothing
but a strategically-placed platter
of gourmet dessert gnats.
Woman who sold her lymph nodes to the sweaty investor.
Woman watching Mars rise low in the swampland dawn,
or Venus, whichever.
Cold-caller extraordinaire. That voice.
Woman as stalagmite, mirror, milliner with a secret
stash of feathers grown from a petri dish
in which the auger is the toe jam
of a boss man.
Radiant as the splendid quetzal.
Not that she is not nullifyingly
defeatingly, negatingly, repeatingly
immediately available to all.

poem puffing up its chest

what are you thinking, always asking, what are you
thinking.   *I'm not*, patiently,
thinking, and still.

just feeling the wind on your face? (demanding)

   Another time I
couldn't speak for forgetting—

You want to be the warm breath of the bumblebee bat on a cold screw
loose in the fortress of empire? Want to lanternfish and radium and
cancer? You want to be bald? Essential? Germ and germination, yellow
bloom of pre-mania, ice on the tender flesh, a tick on the hairline of
complacency? Well, better fucking blow the breath. Do I make you cold?
Do I make you feel? Be, be, be more than I can be, stupid poet; poor,
poor, detritivore—do it! Say it now. I have wasted my life being humble.

—shaking my head to whip it out of me.

This was just a   lesser
      smaller failure.

When my son says I'm a girl and I'm a boy

I'm sitting here pressing on the bump of my nose. My nose—
I keep meaning to figure out which way I need to tilt my head
in photographs, so as not to be photographed
with this bump on my nose.
I can't remember to care long enough, though,
to figure out which angle exactly minimizes
or maximizes my just-so. I feel embarrassed
when I see myself in a picture, but I don't feel embarrassed
when I look in the mirror. Hello, wild thing,
I say; I see you're going with wet bed-head again today.
Thumbs up. Now let's get this party started. I think people
are generally generous toward my presentation.
Actually, I think they don't care. Actually I think they care
about a lot of things. My hair, yes, I know,
it has never looked more like a pair
of cocker spaniel ears, swinging to and fro
in under-washed clumps. Self-deprecation
can be really satisfying. You don't need to tell me I'm not
"that bad." Do you feel frustrated, reader,
by my lack of attendance to my son's early awareness
of the spectrum of gender, the body's ability to be both?
Do you want me to say something to him?
My mom has suggested that I organize a get-together
with some of my daughter's friends and their moms.
All the moms could wear their old prom dresses, she says.
My daughter would love it if I wore my prom dress
to the park. Actually, a few years ago
she would've loved it. Now, I think,
she accepts my disappointing preference for pants
and my sea-green vest over everything,
nine months a year. It's nearly always vest season,
I say, with a little jazz hands. I'll never wear a prom dress
to the coffee shop or to the grocery for her, though
if my son is her, I will do it—I will do it for him.

Clouds

my cloud-potential exists
it's for squeaking my oil can
it's for grasping at
it's for getting wet

I become a sprinkle bear
I become a tangleweed
in relation to a motor
I become a fine mist

cumulonimbus me
I'm a beard, so fleecy—
you can't look at everything
the same, L says, so dark

out some of it, dark
dark & I white it, I white it
dark.   Let's talk some more
about the weather

It's Fine (poem for a windstorm)

It's fine—fine! to wish
for the people with hearts over them
for the people in the potty
who don't want you to poop on them
teacher is not cold
all the friends are ok
your pants are hamburger pants
say, the trees are growing again!
musics will come on:
is it dust? and doglike
cock your head
it can't be seen
it says nothing
cars are rolling down the hill
to wrap themselves in sushi
slap a breast: *is it gentle?*
gentle now, you spackle
in the face of madness
begin a poem
you can go on living
the poem is nothing
can't you make it 'nothing'

TRANS HIMALAYA

I'm walking along, trudging, really, through clumpy grass where slugs drape themselves grossly like used tea bags. I'm thinking of you, "Mister Animal Nut." "Mister Animal Nut," I feel you, stitched to me through an intergalactic web of fantastical proportion. Earlier today I saw a book, titled TRANS HIMALAYA, which I first read as TRASH HIMALAYA, then TRASH IN MALAYSIA, then TRANS IN MALAYSIA. Deep in my interiority, I sometimes feel a dislodging, a slow movement of a wet menace. Would you say, "Mister Animal Nut," that a sickness binds our coasts like a scab? That a flotilla of trash himalayas violently, folding and faulting, composing a continent of waste, an iceberg of itself? We are tethered by a synthetic, a copy, named for nature to further distance us from its actuality. How sinister. I picture you, "Mister Animal Nut," with a kind of squirrel-like face. I believe slugs are common to your area, and the image of a flung tea bag is something to which you can relate. Mammal to mammal, I want to say now, I feel that you know me. Your enthusiasm for the unknown American poet—the way you star her and give her thumbs up—Mister, I don't think you're being ironic. I think you're nuts. . .for *animals*, and I am one, as are you, as is she. Collectively, we're a nebula, an interstellar cloud of dust infused, eachly, with a particular nature of the beast. Let's face it, by which I mean, my face glows in the light of my constellary screensaver. I reflect nothing, and nothing reflects me, nevertheless I beam a feeling, and it moves sluggishly through a smog toward Volans.

Vibrissae

But it's strange to kill / for the sudden feel of life. / The danger is / to moralize / that strangeness. —Robert Hass

Do you know a strangeness deeply or well? I sometimes feel things, as though I too, possess the sensitive vibrissae of a wildebeest or wild boar. I know I don't know you, in the animal sense, or in the sense that we are but friends that haven't yet met, or in the sense that we are twins of light and matter, containers, each, of our highly specific toxic concoctions. *Is* it strange? To kill for the sudden feel of life? One animal supposes. One animal supposes she is on the one hand born to it. Her whittled spines and grinders for tearing and terribly gnashing. Her industrious microbiome. One supposes this is not the whole story. One recalls the domination of flora and fauna, of female beasts like me: the stripping, the naming and caging. The separation of sense from sense. I cannot live with myself. To tear and gnash the flesh of another whom I have not had the will to kill, to eat these bodies and eggs, to prefer breast to leg. And the rest of it—in truth I cannot see the danger of it. Already I kneel down, say: oh hey there, pretty buddy, hey there, good boy.

My Ram Hands

cappuccino-flavored
potato chips &
meaty-textured non-meat
exist, &
wonderpus
photogenicus &
spiny lumpsucker

blobfish exist
my history
of texting, taking pictures
of pages in books
in order
to feel moved again, in order
to feel moved

or in order to stop caring
in order to stop caring
in order to start caring again
it's going to take washing
these ram hands &
knowing they
still smell like ram

another poem that wonders if it feels safer with a blanket over its head

the black scratches   that crumble to ash

what purpose have I   to help myself live

or some 'you'   what ego—

      & by what avenue

      each day a red undulation

that cannot   but must be

to be *made* complicit   is to let—

self: *make* self possess burdens

this one is heavy.   look at it

care for it.   feed it

as an illness,   nothing

that leads to growth   or festering.

feed it as an ascetic, then   with attention.

won't go away.   can't be ignored.

no disguise   no decoration

but must be seen,   as these marks

     in ash must be an I,

asea,   asea

"Who has not broken our heart," said the friend. "Carl Linnaeus has not broken our heart."

The whale-mouse *Balaenoptera musculus* moves like a planet in me. The whale-mouse *Balaenoptera musculus* moves through the same sea that surges in me, the night I bring home *Amos & Boris* and my children are uninterested, so I read it to myself and feel moved on the breach of my couch in the dim living room, feel the mussel in me, feel the pearl. Feel myself a slightly shaky line-drawing of a being bewildered in an ocean that could hold me and drown me, twin me and kin me— vast are the ties that bind, and me, asea—asea! Have you broken my heart, Carl?

*

May I call you Carl, Carl? I am the kind of being who feels unsettled yet and so must amend this proclamation not given to me or for me and you long dead and unable to hear nor care—still, the stethoscope's whooshing confirms my confesh: *whale-mouse* beats the muscle inside of my chest. This twinning spinning out of control, kaleidoscoping until I am—we are—four things, sixteen—what *are* we—wonder, whale, mouse, monster, matter? It's complicated. That's simplistic. I'm simple-minded, but complex-hearted, and I'm bothered, and caught, Carl.

*

In the first edition of *Systema Naturae*, you subdivided the human species into four varieties: "white European," "red American," "brown Asian," and "black African." In the tenth edition of *Systema Naturae* you changed the description of Asian skin tone to "luridus," yellow, and created a 'wastebasket taxon': "monstrosus" for "wild and monstrous humans, unknown groups, and more or less abnormal people." Carl. Have you broken our heart?

*

Your era of collecting and naming, sorting and identifying—it must have been intoxicating. From this era also arose botanical portraits, beautiful portraits that cut off the roots, that erase the sultry breath of jungle or the windswept desert and replace it with a backdrop of airless white, as if we can exist in this blankness of ecology, as if we might want to. Oh, Carl, Carl, I'm itchy, and barnacled, and weak! These glorious mash-ups, these freakish, writhing rubrics in which I mirror myself and mask myself, too—Carl, you must know how divisive, how ruinous we have become. How separately we float from our relations, how lonely this blank backdrop, how ill the four chambers of our tethered hearts.

Deep

I'm a weeping weapon.
I'm a butt catcher.
You're a butt holder.
I'm nuffin. You're Griselda.
You're Danny. Shut it
Danny! You're Warren.
This tank top
w/ the built-in cups—
I'm while. I'm dry
wailing piles.
Houseplant,
dry in the dirt—
be a sister
from another mister.
Have you seen me?
Practicing my sleep moves?
Rub your yucky
little wart foot on my leg,
make me look
at your hangnail.
Tell me about how V died.
Tell me bout when you dived!
I didn't die, honey, I—
Did he go to hospital?
Did he have bloody nose?
Fleshy bracts I pull
you off all air and woo—
B dived.
Yes, she did. B dove.
She dove. I can fit
a whole stuffie in each cup
here's Beastie, here's Teddy
look at this rack
stacked deep!
I'm gonna dive
long time
feel wet in here

an epoch photobombs this selfie

It is like a disposable bag
that catches an updraft
and pulses elegantly.
It is like an empty
Kleenex box
made so by a child
who doesn't know, really
how yet to blow his nose.
It is a plastic assortment
of miniature dogs
grouped according
to who has friends
who is alone.
It's the Boxer.
And some sort of long-hair.
This is the story of the Anthropocene.
It's the story
of the family: monster
tastes like grass
baby monster
crying.
It wants crackers.
I smell meat.
I smell meat in here.

Weapon

It's going to take forever—the rest of our lives, one after another global catastrophe & I'm embarrassed to say in some ways it will be a relief: just end it already, & let the future critters take their wet breaths. The seabird autopsies kill me. I mean they kill everyone—I had vowed to stop saying that things kill me after D asked me if I would kill so-and-so if they did such-and-such minor thing. I can't even remember & it's about killing for godssake. Lately she says to me:

weaponnnnn

in a whispery, sinister voice & it chills me, Jesus Christ it chills me. I ask her, what is a weapon & she replies it is something that flies through the air, my friends play it at school:

weaponnnnn

I'm not one I create what nature does better—evolve or metastasize to block the sun, that thing, that thing—that toothless teratoma ellenwelcker, that hairball in the drain, ellenwelcker, that three year-old is an intertextual act of radical social action   she's politeness theory she's a bat poet   she's lonely she's a few feet away   floating in a sea   of plastic debris with a blowhole big enough for a baby to crawl through. O, to throw out your nasty ole ratty ass sweatpants & have a whale swallow them, now this makes me want to die

Alright

—after Paisley Rekdal's "The Wolves"

It was the night of histrionics. Histrionics
over everything, *probably just tired.*
She'd had a really good day. We know
what that's like. You blink, blink and think this
is alive. But only after. In the good day,
you're just in it. Then sobbing. Don't wanna
grow up. Wish I were his age. *Wish
I could stay with you, and we didn't have
to die or knew*—I moved in the space
between shushing and the lie.

The lie has felt more truthful lately.
There have been times when I couldn't.
I felt a jinx lurk, felt its hunger. The oldest fear:
of not knowing if I would be able to keep her safe,
what that betrayal might look like for her,
in the rest of her days. It was too much.
I said nothing. Or said, *we can't know, and this
is the blah blah blah of alive.*
Listened, mute, to a spirit come howling
into a small and pitiful creature.

Now I say *hush*, I say the we can't know part,
the blah blah blah part. I say *big feelings*,
and *with you*, and *feel them*. And I say it's alright.
Which bewilders me. I say *alright, alright, it's
alright* and I don't mean "it" and I don't
mean "right," just a kind of hum
that's an aaah I can get behind. I say crazy
ass shit like *never gonna leave you* and
always be with you, and I don't worry
about the hungry jinx.

When she gets a little older, I will give her
a mad-eyed smile. I'll put my stone cold finger

in her sternum and say, *I will HAUNT you,*
and she will laugh and shake her head.
But even at six she knows. My cells
her blood my dust her hair my breath.
Her lungs. I'm not leaving.
It was a good day.
And other things, too. What
is the difference now.

It's Called the Sea

A tiny kitten scratches my palm. Later I find the claw embedded like a pearl or a fossil in the meat of me. I give a puppy a bloody nose that won't stop. That night I blow up the American buffalo. I push it off a cliff. It's my anniversary. I don't want this to be about me. I heave a beached orca into a plastic bag. It quietly doubles over on itself. I twist the top of the bag and look for a bread tie. There is none to be found. I push it out into collective shame and anxiety. It's called the sea. My name is unpronounceable. The whale's name is whale.

II. Mouth That Tastes of Gasoline

Mouth That Tastes of Gasoline

1.

it's hard to find a living person

hard not to Google the others, their blogs so polished . . .

it's weird when people use Facebook to communicate
with the dead but I get it:

the way humans evolve to carry useless organs around

I'm a machine with my own colossal network
the small print: it's a beak in my hearts
it's weird

when you're asked

to check yes or no

I know

the world prefers me

bewildered

2.

the way humans evolve to carry useless organs around

saying, I am the ticket
'til rubble fills the throat they come
clotted & pieced. I know:

"you're at home with the soft leopards"
"you should be in a tent"
"you should be getting your tent removed"

someone slits
cuts & pulls

to loosen I

gill-less slithering I

"had a simple air sac beneath my throat"
"something suitable"
"for real-world problem solving"

hot & bloody hot & bloody
I loose this body I loose this body

fetal the memory of sheer amassed tonnage
the beached aggregations

the only wholly imaginable key to a valueless net worth
a vascular alternative to a machine

dear flapping & whumping
in my queer & ordinary heart,

the way humans evolve to burst out of their forms—

tell yourself to be careful
then do the thing that's danger

that's an example of a conversation
between powerful beings in charge

3.

to be continued, to be continued
    the bracketed world

    that must be unstapled

the way humans evolve to suck sweetness through straws
    the way humans evolve to salt the food

    "like a complicated thing"   "that prefers to live simply"

the dismal niche screaming *shellfish*
    & bathing its faces in the sun

    a conjunctive mourning

in the collective unconscious

4.

one thing we found was the map
so beloved, & beloved, the lines were all wrong

like the leashburn sustained in one's nostril
while hogtied & holding the baby
the advice, so difficult
to read

until slowly, slowly,
one reads
about dancing

with the man in the man-suit too short
in the legs, in the cathedral of night crawlers,
spineless, goodbye

pitbull in a shopping cart outside 7-Eleven, goodbye
penchant for wanton & earthly things

(like that list
of our losses
salad spinner,
I don't miss you)

the way humans evolve to rummage in basements
saying, where is the container
for all of the new blood?
the yins dividing up language & things
the yangs dividing up language & things

meticulous dividing of language & things
into boy parts & girl parts
boy things & girl things

some things outnumbering
vastly outnumbering

5.

lament as a matter of deep relativity
disclaimer in emphatic relation

the way turtles   are bound by their
skeletons to their shells
& an algal bloom   gets in the nostrils
        plugs

lament
disclaimer
landfill as dinner

a vascular mind in a vascular room
a mind machine in a room full of breathing

lifting one's breath above one's flapping & whumping . . .

parting from one's flapping & whumping . . .

queer & ordinary heart:
the way humans evolve to desire a man
whose mouth tastes of gasoline

6.

lifting one's breath . . .
parting from one's breath . . .

& the pressure necessary to winch
to winch! to winch!

the winching required of the hands   the hands
so open at rest   clenched!   clenched!

the flecks of graciousness
thrown back untasted

the empty cages, picturesque, &
the birds that flit about   unnamed   desirable

the collective & unconscious mourning
of species by objectification

& the very, very
shiny shoes . . .

the go or stay of the party
the now or later of the party
to come & whether one's attendance
is in question
is in question

the way humans
evolve
to be covetous
of feathers

7.

I say like too much
I say it like 25 times
so just-home, so gushy

"the small plates, so delicious"

"the earrings, so twinkly"

the statement
it flushes, I go
to wash dishes

the way humans evolve to say they weren't born for this

the way humans evolve to say they weren't born for this

ass tattoo is a
sparrow / swallow?

sky brother
so gone

in a canyon

heart come out mouth
            on fire

                        & my mouth

        that tastes of gasoline

8.

the way humans evolve into orifice upon orifice
the way humans evolve to say they weren't born for this

how she wore a slinky dress
slippery
dangerous

like a cormorant
or a mother

you want to confirm
a controversial statement
with a kiss?

tell yourself to be careful
then do the thing
that's danger

you're an animal whose
face looks to be smiling

this is an example of a conversation
between powerful men
in charge:

"vast & intimate knowledge of minutiae"
(devastating reminder of the evolution of evolution)

pry it back
pry it back

the myth of the newborn takes nothing
of this bloody world into account

the baby says something
& I say it back
how I say it to her
& she says it back

it is her thinking that stars are little moons
it is the monster telling her no
holes
all bunched up in the middle

9.

disclaimer

the way humans evolve to dredge & truck
            toxin & dioxin
all the beaches

screaming   shellfish
don't eat the

            shellfish

poor shellfish   everyone

bringing cream puffs & souvenir key chains
bringing vast & intimate knowledge

of some of the minutiae

            but not all of the minutiae
            not bird names

the hair that keeps growing
the nails that keep growing

the teeth that keep growing & growing & growing

            landfill as dinner

the very shiny shoes &
the absentminded   tonguing
            of olives

the marshmallow whip
mistaken   for mayonnaise
the salad plate
            a homunculus pile

pollen counts are high
schistosomiasis exists
       as do people

who don't wash their hands satisfactorily

the buffet
eternally synonymous
w/ particulate,   suspended
       particulate, gleaming

like a bird, you celebrate
       at all the wrong times
like a bird, you shit
       without aiming, die

in oil slicks, cause me endless
       distress over those plastic
six-pack holders, me—me!
       then you fly

& fly & fly & fly & fly & fly

10.

oh, to speak of dying
or mold

to speak of moles
sharks, or crashing

to cry out, noisily
with regard to

spiders, scorpions or
darkness

pathogens, generally or
pathogens, specifically

commitment, nuclear
winter,

heavy objects
precarious

Hanta virus
a queer flumping, or whapping

the cormorant
does not look threatening

it is drying its wings
its wings

its creepy, slick wings
the way humans

evolve
to desire a man

whose mouth tastes
of gasoline

11.

to speak of humiliation
intestinal disorders or

fissures, imagined or real
disfiguring facial tumors

the collapse of colony
or emotional I-beams

the question: is it viral?
the question: are you coming?

to speak of mental illness
or a problem with the rheum

to shout "fungus," "unseemly
rash," "boredom" or

unsure what exactly—
stay away from the shellfish

maybe, or don't lock your knees
always take the stairs—

to bawl about gas leaks, public
restrooms, strange

odors, or sprue—to speak of swine flu
or pink eye, no not pink eye

a conjunctive unconscious
collectively mourning,

all gunked up, gross
an inability to render

or recall, to never
have learned

yet to speak
of imminent or hypothetical acts

of terrorism, to cry out
noisily, with regard to beards

other people's blood, old food
oddly colored passports

to shout "tomorrow," "scurvy"
"capability, comma, illusion of"

"paralysis, comma, partial or full"
is it viral, are you coming

are you drying your wings
are you creepy, slick, or black

does it pale you
where you keep your organs

they bubble when I lie
they are softest

when I am disoriented
try to think of me

as the cupcake
of the sea

bred for qualities
deemed appealing

our +1
is kissing the remote control

& conjuring devastating reminders
of the evolution of evolution

12.

the enormous
piano that causes an epiphany

(one doesn't process music appropriately)
        (one is not properly moved)

one doesn't comprehend
magnitude

the magnitude of what it is
        to build a grand piano in one's mind

all clutching our keys
& pressing

our navels together
        ass tattoo

is a hummingbird?
starthroat?

tell yourself you are beautiful
        then flush

bye-bye prescriptions
toxin & dioxin

the beaches cormoranted
        or plugged

osmotic & dear
it's so clear

13.

lead with the fist & skull
like a goat or a unicorn

     the way humans evolve to disappear amphibians, & each other

to spit & lick on this weaponry
shining them shining them shining

     so stuck in these forms

take to gesture & gadgetry
sniffing & rummaging, liking & messaging

     the way humans evolve to save the proofs of their purchases

say you love freedom
look away from the man holding your safe word ransom

     that's an example of a conversation

between power darlings
a most oppressive thing

     to be predisposed to delusion

dear flapping & whumping in my queer
& ordinary heart

     I said our +1 is kissing the remote control

14.

a plan of time that turns into a wrong turn
a wrong turn that turns into a series of tumors
tumors that must be cut out or ground in

the way humans evolve to forage in hog parts

the offal, the offal, & on the radio
statistics, statistics about underdogs

the way humans evolve to lump & tumesce
the way humans evolve to exact & excise

to dredge & truck & burst from our forms
to feel safe in our cars

& to fall in love
with a man

whose mouth smells like Valvoline

pry it back
            to be continued

pry it back
            to be continued

the way humans evolve to plunder the orifice
that's an example of a conversation

between predators, & a very
deep empathy within us for underdogs

15.

do you ever think (trying
to remember)

answer "yes"
or "no"

a nagging feeling
wasn't there

wasn't there something else
something streaming

in the blue semi-consciousness of hand
rubbing back, the swift kick

in the turtle meat of me
the brightness

of thought that is unbringbackable
what sits in a box

hurts me from the box
& I feel so close

to some bronze baboons
all burnished by the laying of hands

16.

our safe word was
platypus

our token word was
prehensile tail
so easily
mixed up

(it was a time
just before
this particular strain
would enter
the collective
conjunctive)

17.

a clownish word means
"to belong to me"

some spastic neural pathway
or insistence on a thinkership

in which commodities could speak
in which I am a failure

of crypto-representational proportions
a failure to grapple with

my interiority has been compromised
my markets have been encroached upon

to what degree no one will say
perhaps my fission mouth will say

perhaps my winter mouth, my
coal shaft mouth, my high-value target

mouth, my ideology mouth + my highway
mouth my friction mouth gap mouth alliance mouth

my body mouth my commodity mouth
I'm speaking of course with my terrorist mouth

my prayerist mouth. my viable mouth. my undesirable
mouth. my blood-egg mouth. my occupied mouth. my apocalypse
mouth my colony collapse mouth my ruthlessly self-critical mouth
my possibility mouth. I'm speaking with my we
mouth. my self + self mouth
my self + self + self mouth

18.

this is a workbook
you can write in it

how she wore a slinky dress
slippery, dangerous

like a mother can be
you can watch

a cruise ship slide by
while stuck in the underpass

you can watch a man left open
he is a hand-crank music box

you can see an email left open
the subject is mother love

the subject is penguins
the subject is pink dots, wild

here is a girl's job
it is looking for snails outside

don't forget your snailbag!
it is an earthquake that happens

while you are talking about nothing
but not a bit of umbilicus that hangs on

& eventually lets go of its scar
it is her thinking that stars are little moons

it is the monster telling her no, suns
everyone holding the hostess

& pressing their navels together
the way humans evolve to be

predisposed to delusion: tell yourself
to be careful

then do the thing that's danger
that's an example of a conversation

between executives
o, the small

insurrections
of my face

19.

my face
my face
doing oratory practice in the ghost-child's bedroom

my face dreaming
of something disturbing:
a statue of a face or a big-lunged man

bye-bye statue, bye-bye face
I knit a bit of ash, a bit of cement, I knit
a bit of bone

for the big-lunged man
the lungs, ingenious
regenerate, the way humans evolve

to open secret spaces
vestibules or black boxes
in which tiny souls lie slick

& fetal, viscous & bright as spawn
eye of hurricane, hole of gone
bigger, & stickier—the seen

then unseen
my face dreams of something
disturbing: wakes

to find the ghost-child eating dirt
in the sideyard singing bye-bye gargoyles
& gnashing her lungs

20.

lead with fist & skull, revolutionaries
like a revolutionary narwhal

the way humans evolve to spray germs
on everyone & other

the way we spit & lick on this weaponry
shining them, shining them, shining

the myth of the newborn takes nothing
of this bloody world into account

the little cilia working
& the nuclei bursting, bursting

how the baby says something
& I say it back

how I say it to her
& she says it back

it is her thinking that stars are little moons
& the monster telling her no, diamonds

then guillotined, guillotined—o
the monster—the baby—the microbe

guillotined—see?
the clean symmetry?

of flagella or twisted tooth
the orbiting vessels of monster or microbe

dilate, dilate
the horn-crossed heart is encased

in a skin so blue, it's hard, hard
in a skin so blue, it's hard

21.

the way humans evolve
to suck on each others' flesh

the music that causes a quick
emotion to happen, attached

to people—quite naturally / sleep
in the flesh, the flesh my body

of flesh amassed implies
a humbling network of touching
& sloughing, feeling & roughing

impossible to deny a body
climbing in, in with the music
that makes us fall asleep

or beg, beg, or die hollering:
take my mouth away

or open it up to cake
or bodies   the parts all saying *schwah*

& flailing around in their flesh

> embarrassing humans—follicular humans—the way we
> hear things—always sounding—& caught
> in the microfiche—boss-laden & strewn—pliant
> & tendrilled—in awkward positions—exceedingly
> awkward positions

though I've spent time in this one
millennia in this one

I'm still so strangled & clutchy
of the Hostess cream-filled cakes

& looking to press with someone
these wrinkled navels together

Notes

"A white cry brought the morning to its feet": Italicized lines are Federico García Lorca's, from *Poet in New York* (The Noonday Press, 1998), translated by Greg Simon and Steven F. White. This poem was originally published in *Verde Que Te Quiero Verde: Poems After Federico García Lorca*, published by Open Country Press, 2016. Thank you Natalie Peeterse.

Lines in "Still Life with Viewer as Object" are from Joanna Newsom's song, "Divers": 'the nullifying, defeating, negating, repeating joy of life.'

"Clouds" is for Lauren Campbell.

"Vibrissae" is for Holly Amos.

"My Ram Hands" is after Inger Christensen.

"'Who has not broken our heart,' said the friend. 'Carl Linnaeus has not broken our heart'" is for and after Kathryn Nuernberger.

Acknowledgments

I'm grateful to the editors at *Pinwheel, Willow Springs, small po[r]tions, Horse Less Review, Open Country Press, Similar Peaks, JERRY, Everyday Genius, Phantom, Indigest* and *Matter Monthly* for publishing some of these poems, often as younger versions of themselves. *Mouth That Tastes of Gasoline* was previously published as a chapbook in the Shotgun Wedding Series (alice blue, 2014). Thanks to Amber Nelson.

Thanks to Sharma Shields, friend and mentor, for relentless championship of my poems, and for taking on this project. Thanks to Maya Jewell Zeller for generous editorial assistance and open invitations to kayak, to Keely Honeywell for her gorgeous design work, to many friends who helped these poems germ and germinate including Maya, Laura Read, Kathryn Smith, Kathryn Nuernberger, Ellie Kozlowski, Torrey Smith, Rachel Mehl, Thom Caraway, Jeff Dodd, Kris Dinnison, Kevin Taylor, Shann Ray Ferch, Eli Francovich, and to the warm and wonderful literary community of Spokane. Thank you especially to friends and family who brought this project into being with generous donations of cold hard cash and endless love. Thank you Shannon, Peter, and Dad for the gift of writing space, to Zach for ongoingness and thank you to Jacob for uttering the phrase in the first place.

This book is for Clyde.

About the Author

Ellen Welcker's obsessions include ecological desperation, boundaries real and imagined, and the concept of deep humanity as an animal state. Her first book, *The Botanical Garden* (Astrophil Press, 2010), was selected by Eleni Sikelianos for the Astrophil Poetry Prize in 2009. Chapbooks include *Mouth That Tastes of Gasoline* (alice blue books, 2014) and *The Urban Lightwing Professionals* (H_NGM_N, 2011). She lives in Spokane, WA, with her family, and works for the Bagley Wright Lecture Series on Poetry.